Traitorous Muse

Brooke Gross

Presentation by *BookLeaf Publishing*

Web: www.bookleafpub.com

E-mail: info@bookleafpub.com

ISBN: 9789395621144

First edition 2022

DEDICATION

This book is dedicated to the lives unlived, the words unsaid, and the people unfortunate enough to remember them. May we make peace with the muses that terrify us.

ACKNOWLEDGEMENT

I first have to thank my husband, who is so wonderful that I will never be able to accurately portray him with mere words. This project also wouldn't have been possible without my family; I'm extremely blessed that you have always supported my writing. Lastly, I want to thank the teachers and mentors who have helped me grow over the years.

The Siren's Spiral

Beware the muse
the candle warned
on brightest summer morning
for stillest seas
still toss at night
but sailors never frighten

I listen well
avoid shipwreck
but oh how pages beckon
blank and pure
starved of ink
and now my ship is sinking

Lucifer smiled
so I forgot
the halo dead and rotting
the feathers black
the star that fell
the love that turned to hellfire

I do my best
to close my eyes
but darkness feels so silky
wrapped in dreams
thick as smoke
and now my angel's choking

Whatever Lyricism Is

A mountain of pages on the floor
A river of ink in my head
A guitar in my hand
Just wish I knew what it said
Roll your name over my tongue
to see how you taste
in a love song
to see if you deserve my good grace

There's an army outside
but a lock on the door
There's a secret I'm hiding
about the night before
I burned all your pictures
built a house of charred matches
I put up a smoke screen
to watch you sift through the ashes

A little girl in the corner
A teddy bear in the rain
A rescue party coming in
if she could remember his name
If her innocence was spared
maybe the pain would be gone
but they'll reopen the wounds
to hear a whisper of her song

Fireflies and Fairytales

Mississippi skies
streaked with heat lightning
like climate cries
and systemic disappointment
tampered only by the heavy chill
of heartless mediocrity

Alabama skies
cloud-covered by grief
of Birmingham-born bloodlines
roots too deep to untangle
pulled up by weary dreamers
back down by drug and drink

Georgia skies
like Christmas lights
white bulbs dangle
from black thread
air slick with the sweat
of colorblind devils

Louisiana skies
over voodoo haze
gothic horror and iron gates
gators and sinking swamps

don't bite unless provoked
whisper hurricane curses

Florida skies
half heaven, half hill
hybrid culture for heathen hearts
summer rain sings
magic marred only by capitalist
fear of a setting sun

Gambling in the Heartland

5

You thought you were in God's hands
when you chose to duel the devil
but Eve had many enemies
and fiddles don't play like they used to

You thought he had an angel's wings
but shadows can be deceiving
halos, hellfire, and Edison's bulbs
all glisten, gold and gleaming

Made a Friend in Sin City

I could ask you a question
only you'll understand
lay cards on the table
risk showing my hand

I'm holding aces and hearts
you've got a tarot card deck
We were rigged long ago
What's left to reset?

The Joker plays for fun.
The Voodoo Man rolls fake dice.
The Dealer should be on guard.
The Queen tries to play nice.

I go by old habits
whispers of danger
You go by old riddles
just to test my anger

I'd level the minefield
with rules we're breaking
if I knew your game better
Is the risk worth taking?

Crave

is a dirty word
born of sin
and poor impulse control

mouth-watering
seduction
a gut feeling gone wrong

a lonely crime
tasteless fruit
a chaste kiss and starved moan

the secrecy
found in lust
and around dark places

battle of wills
devolving
into an all-out war

a hopeless heart
a lucid dream
a lit fuse with no end

My Bartender is My Sponsor

I've been clean
for almost a decade
At least, that's what he thinks
but burning liquid luck
was never my preferred drink

It's the menace
in his jawline
that keeps me sober now
If he only knew his eyes
were enough to make me drown

He's been stoned
since the day he met me
high on being wanted
but love couldn't wake him up
so we both go home haunted

It's the fever
in my musings
that keeps him standing still
pretends I'm not his weakness
wonders of whiskey and will

We were ruined
before we started
broken lonely addicts
I still cook with alcohol
He takes exposure tactics

The Friendship Test

"You'll get hurt," he said.
"I want to try," she implored.
"You can't do this," he insisted.
but she'd opened the door

Love and lust aren't the same.
Love and friendship? Please.
No two virtues
are greater enemies.

She wore the uniform well
buttons all in a row.
Even with a lonely heart
held her X's and O's.

"What game are you playing?"
he wants to know
"Nothing," she swears.
"Harmless flirting! A joke!"

He'll never trust her
but he's drawn to the thrill.
Who doesn't love a girl
that just can't get her fill?

Down the trapdoor they go
again and again.
She'll flash a clever smile.
He'll feel guilty as sin.

testing testing
on your knees
sidestep the pain
by the skin of your teeth

"I was kidding myself."
"I wanted you too."
"You never said anything."
"What good would it do?"

If you're thinking of someone
you've already failed.
Welcome to purgatory
this platonic jail.

Blueberry Cobbler

Coffee in a pot
but no one to drink
tears on a girl's face
it's not what you think

Books on computers
how academics fall
reach for high and pride
just to get through it all

Someone's wedding
follows one last kiss
when nights go to hell
it's not love you miss

Family meeting
get our story straight
nothing lasts forever
coffee's burned anyway

Would I Run to You?

in the field of forgotten flowers
I torched
when I found the poison
under your bed
my safe place
my soft place
my dandelion wishes
ablaze with red-hot fury
dead blooms left stiff
in your cold calculation

in the haunted house
I built for you
with bricks you'd made
pretty paint you'd mixed
in the field of ash
and flame-blue weeds
roots as strong as the floorboards
you nailed too deep
I can't pull up
but at least you're only a ghost

in the daydreams and nightmares
that say too much of impermanence
ramble with afterthoughts

what if
could have been
I know better
but subconscious is fickle
can't control walking sleep
lost desire - unmet wishes
and what of the waking world

in the poems on paper
I wish I could shred
fuck you
my muse
reluctant yet unyielding
too beautifully broken
to give up
not mine to keep
Would I sprint through the sharp-tongued
papercuts anyway?

On the Tip of Your Tongue

Almost is a
prayer
sent to hell
instead of heaven

Almost is a
wish
on a star
that fell back to earth

Almost is an
oops
never should
and never will be

Almost is an
out
if you fear
the threat of always

Almost is just
enough
of love
to know
what you crave

Heads or Tails

The backwoods self-made without a cause
took a trip to the bayou in a gator's jaws
With a fishing net and a rusty pole
caught a few crawfish in a muddy hole
Watched the sun set in a cloud of green
happy with an airboat and somewhere to lean

The outcast, now more than he ever thought
put two tires to the road, grabbed a camera, took
off
Met a witch under neon lights
looked to the stars, but couldn't find the sky
For crazy fans and city love
found something more than someone else's stuff

The queen in heels and airbrush pink
carved perfect circles in biker ink
Started an empire on beauty and curls
paving pretty power for kick-ass girls
Got thrown some beads on a nameless street
can't blame the boys for the bourbon heat

The coin that cuts through eclectic air
makes a corner of the world neither here nor
there

Tells one side of a story in jazz and tattoos
another in camo and a swamp-grown muse
With art in the Quarter and smoke in the alley
always something to love and something to rally

Willow Wounds

I sat beneath a tree today
almost as sad as me
she hid it well
her scars were hell
but branches kept on swaying

the veil of leaves I slipped between
spoke low and soft and rough
they asked me why
do angels cry
when demons call them beloved

"it isn't real," I told the roots
no matter what they do
real love can leave
still hate can grieve
she sighed, "if only you knew"

I Know Better

Watch your step
in the haunted house
blood stains deeper
in a hollow heart

Hold your breath
on the ocean floor
black sand sparkles
but the offer's cursed

Don't move a muscle
under lover's touch
teeth get sharper
with a lonely tongue

Don't get lazy
in the demon's dance
wicked words sing
to a racing pulse

But I'm too familiar
with the kisses of ghosts
to remember the sounds
of shipwreck and loss

Purge

Summer rain
reminds me
that beautiful days
still cry

Summer rain
teaches me
that even the sun
can bleed

Summer rain
betrays me
a comfort
and a mess

Summer rain
surrounds me
with heaven's pity
and devil's wrath

Still

You lie tranquil now
dormant as a winter rose
He watches soft sighs
with bated breath
I wait for the trembling
I knew instead

He feels gentle touch
smooth strokes
calligraphic sonnets
I know fingers in my hair
guiding over stick shift
frantic script and bloody ink
drumming on my chest
willing my heart to beat
in time with yours

He hears whispers of affection
murmurs of desire
I flinch at sobs of desperation
begging me to love you

He has words of affirmation
silent support

promising demure
I have shouts of triumph and terror
sworn "I don't need you"s
sonic echoes of my rejection

He thinks you still
but I remember your screams

Silent

I have known
a quiet love
that creeps in shadows
and lives in bone

I have known love
so secret and soft
you never knew
if it was real or not

I have heard
the whispered words
hidden in the breeze
trapped behind lips

I have heard words
devoted and true
against my skin
yet not in his head

I have seen
a breaking heart
too composed to show
behind stained glass

I have seen hearts
well matched in the dark
cooling comfort
over blazing fire

I have felt
a silent love
but what I want
is the one that screams

You'd Never Know

You'd never know
two days ago
there were demons in my head
The sun would rise
on kitchen knives
to dot my bath mat red

You'd never know
two weeks ago
there was violence in my eyes
The lock would turn
while pages burn
love like lust and lies

You'd never know
two months ago
there was nothing left to learn
The spark would drown
no body found
in tears you didn't earn

You'd never know
two years ago
there was mischief all around
The flowers bloomed

in warm high-noon
to greet a cheerful town

You'd never know
mere moments ago
I'd forgotten the incident
The scars are thin
but second sin
holds out for heaven-sent

Tiptoe

Raise to pointe
"How is your wife?"
Pirouette
"She's doing fine."

Balance beam
"I like your work."
Tightrope walk
Love must be earned.

Eggshell steps
Don't go too far.
Paper cuts
"It's been too long."

Head of pin
"So is it true?"
Needle thread
"I missed you too."

On the edge
"He's lucky, Brooke."
Riddle read
"I wrote a book."

Perilous Interpretations

when ink bleeds
through pages
smears beyond
fine lines
stains hands
off guard
soaks deep
into spines
of books
it doesn't
belong to

What, then, is the difference
between a love letter and hate mail?

when words choke
like a vice
poison polite
conversation
stick to skin
like ash
wake dead
dreams denied
burrow deep
into souls
unwilling

Tell me, then,
is the author or reader to blame?

The Places I Once Loved

I don't know when exactly I became
a runaway
the first time I gave into this incessant
urge to escape
when I began writing love letters in blood
to places I thought
would remember me

I can't remember when I discovered
that getting lost
was a luxury
that my new scars would greet nostalgia
like a long lost
bottle of antiseptic

I don't know when I realized I wanted
someone to look for me
the first time I wrote a riddle
just to see who'd bother
to solve it
when I started to wonder if not coming
back was the only way to know